THE TRUTH ABOUT THE MOON

Clayton Bess

THE TRUTH ABOUT THE
MOON

Illustrated by Rosekrans Hoffman

Macmillan/McGraw-Hill School Publishing Company
New York Chicago Columbus

For information regarding permission, write to
Houghton Mifflin Company
2 Park Street
Boston, Massachusetts 02108

This edition is reprinted by arrangement with
Houghton Mifflin Company

Macmillan/McGraw-Hill School Division
10 Union Square East
New York, New York 10003

Printed in the United States of America
ISBN 0-02-274920-9

6 7 8 9 RRC 99 98 97 96 95

For Bess and Clay,
more than a mother and father,
warm, understanding, loving –
teachers too,
the most generous.

– C.B.

For Bob

– R.H.

Sumu grabbed for the moon. Missed it. Then, as fast and high as a hare, he leaped for it. Still it floated just beyond the reach of his fingertips.

That little moon! What a puzzlement! It followed him around like a dog, always just over his shoulder, yet it had the face of a person. Sometimes it was big and round; at other times small and thin; then gone completely. Now here it was back again, very, very thin, only a crescent. But as bright as ever, shiny as silver in the sun. And Sumu wanted it!

"Fatu," he said to his big sister who was plaiting her friend Lorpu's hair. "Please hand me down that baby moon there."

"Heedle dee hee hee!" the two girls put their heads together and giggle-gaggled. Sumu could not see the humor.

"You silly," Fatu said. "It's too high."

"How high?"

"As high as . . . higher even than the treetops, you silly. Besides, what would you do with it?"

"I will put it in a bottle."

"Gabbledy gluggle!" laughed the girls.

"And tomorrow night when this baby moon's bigger brother comes to follow me around the town, I will catch him too and put him in the bottle. And the next night, their sister. And all their brothers and sisters every night until I have the whole moon family in my bottle. Then I will have their light always."

"You silly-silly! There is only one moon. This I know, for our pa told me so."

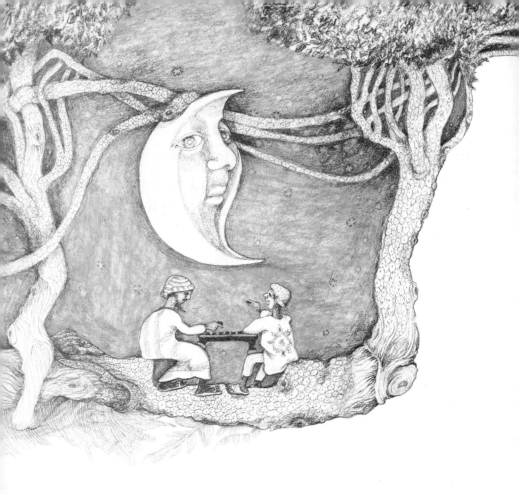

Some nights passed, and now the moon was altogether different, grown to half. Sumu had puzzled
and puzzled over what Fatu had said, and now he
brought the matter to his pa, who was playing
checkers with his good friend Fayah. And losing.

"Pa," Sumu began, "I know now there is only one moon, but . . ."

"Ha hardee hardee ha!" laughed Pa.

"Lak lak lak lak lak!" laughed Fayah. Sumu waited for them to stop. What was so funny, anyway?

"Only one moon!" Pa said finally. "No, Sumu, there are many, many moons."

"But Pa . . ."

"Now this moon you see tonight," Pa went on as though Sumu had not spoken, "is the same moon you saw last night and the same moon you will see tomorrow night. It is growing, just as a child like you grows to be a man like me. It starts small, just a silver sliver, and every night grows bigger and bigger until it is as big as it can be, a full circle. Then, just as a man grows smaller when he is very old, so does the moon. Smaller and smaller until death. And then it is dark of the moon. Then out comes a new baby moon, born to start it all over again. This I know because my pa told me so."

Hmmmmm, Sumu thought. Then he said, "But Pa, where does the new moon come from?"

"Well, uh . . ."

"And where does it go during the day?"

"Well, uh . . ."

"And why does—?"

"Oh, because that's the way it is!" Pa barked. "Can't you see I'm busy with Fayah? Don't bother me now with your silly questions."

More nights passed with Sumu puzzling over what his pa and sister had said. Now the moon had waxed to full, and Sumu brought it to his ma, who was fanning rice with her good friend Goma. It tagged along just over his shoulder and threw its light down on the three of them.

"Ma," Sumu began, "I know now there are many, many moons, but . . ."

"Hoo hooroo hooroo hoo!" laughed Ma.

"Deedle deedle deedle!" laughed Goma. Sumu waited patiently. He was used to getting laughed at now.

"Many, many moons!" Ma finally said when she collected her breath again. "No, Sumu, there is only one moon. It is like a woman. And you know how sometimes a woman will grow larger and larger, more and more round?"

"Yes," Sumu answered.

"And then she will go away for several days, and when she comes back . . . ?"

"She is thin again," Sumu finished for her.

"That's right. And she has—?"

"A baby!" Sumu cried, wondering why he had not understood it all before.

"And so it is with the moon, Sumu. This I know, for my ma told me so."

Hmmmmm, Sumu thought. Then he said, "But Ma, where is the moon's baby?"

the moon is
mother,
moon
her

"Well, uh . . . in the sky! We call them stars. Every month the moon hangs a new baby star in the sky."

"But Ma, if the moon is the mother, who is the father?"

"Well, uh . . . the sun!"

"The sun is the father? But Ma, the sun is hot. The moon and stars are cold. Why?"

"Oh, because that's the way it is!" Ma snapped. "Can't you see I'm busy with Goma? Don't bother me now!"

And then the moon waned to gibbous. Sumu
knew it would get smaller and smaller until it was
gone altogether. And still he had no answers. So
he went to the Chief. The Chief would know. He
was always right, everyone said so, for he was the
wisest man in the village, perhaps even in all Africa.

As Sumu made his way across the village to the
Chief's house, he tried his best to trick his friend
the moon. He ducked under the thatch of an over-
hanging roof to give the moon the slip. But when
he looked out from under the thatch, there was the
moon watching him, waiting for him to come out
again. He jumped into the jungle. But up through
the leaves and fronds, up among the coconuts, he
could see that old moon floating above, spying on
his every move. Sumu had to admit it: That little
moon was very cunning!

Sumu came at last to the Chief's house, the moon still dogging him. The Chief was sitting back in his chair, gazing up at the dark sky, watching for shooting stars.

"Old Pa?" Sumu said to the Chief.

"Hmmm?"

Sumu had so many questions by now, it was hard to choose where to start. Finally he said, "Old Pa, why is the moon cold and the sun hot?"

The Chief looked down at Sumu with very wise and very, very old eyes, eyes as bright as half-sucked pieces of dark sugar candy held up to the sun. He did not laugh.

"You have always asked questions, isn't it so, Sumu? Did your ma ever tell you the first word you ever spoke?"

"No."

"Was it 'Ma' or 'Pa' or any of the words any other child would speak first? No. You said 'Why?'"

"Why?"

The Chief laughed. "I don't know why! Because you were born curious, it seems. But anyway, about the moon . . ."

"Yes, Old Pa?"

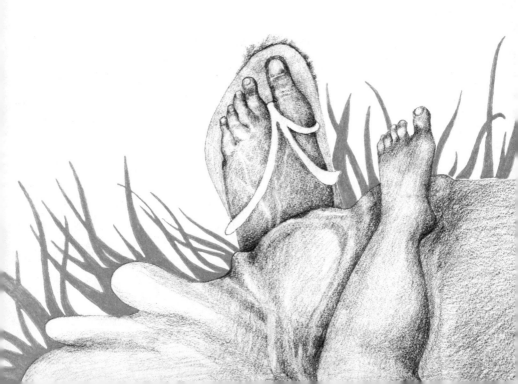

"You asked a very good question, and I will give you a very good answer. Sit down here on my knee and listen well."

Sumu sat down with satisfaction. At last he was getting somewhere.

"Now I know this is so," the old man began, "because my pa told me so. And his pa told him, and his pa before him told him. Once upon a time . . ."

"Time," Sumu responded, following the custom in their town to begin a tale with an echo of time.

". . . the sun and the moon were happily married. All day long they would shine together on the earth, and at night they would go to sleep at the same time. But all night long, then, there would be a deep, dreadful blackness on earth, and poor Man could not move out of his house for fear of getting lost. So Man appealed to the sun and the moon, crying out to them in his frail voice, 'Oh please, Mr. Sun and Mrs. Moon, give us some light at night so we don't have to be afraid.'

"The sun and the moon considered this problem, and they decided that he would shine all day and she would shine all night so that Man would not have to be afraid of the dark.

"Now at this time the sun and moon were both very bright and both were equally hot. So with the sun watching over Man all day and the moon all night, the night was just as bright and hot as the day. You couldn't tell where day left off and night began.

"Man was not happy with this new arrangement. Not at all! He couldn't sleep. Always either the sun or the moon was shining in his eyes. Not only that, but it was always hot. The earth never had a chance to cool off. The ground became dry and the crops began to die.

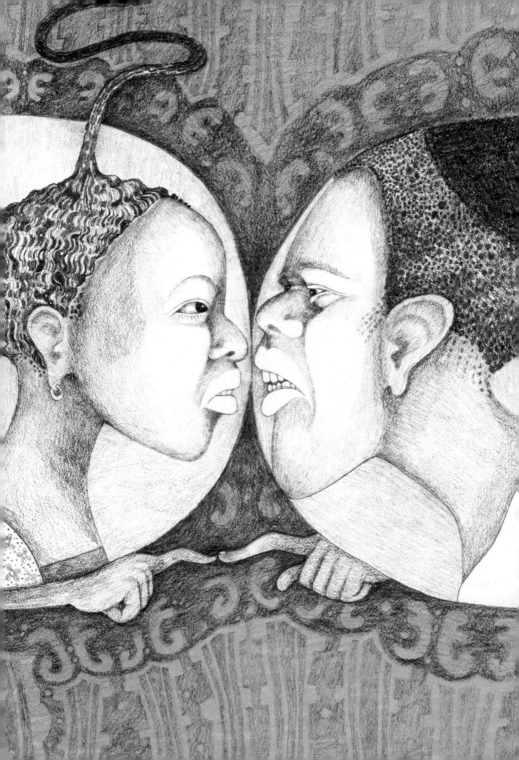

"'Oh, Mr. Sun and Mrs. Moon,' cried Man. 'Please do something. We can't sleep, and it is always hot, and our crops are drying up.'

"'Yes,' said the sun, 'and I'm not happy either. I never see my wife anymore. When I am shining, she is sleeping; when she is shining, I am sleeping. Come, my dear,' he said to the moon, 'let's go back to our old ways and shine together all day and sleep at night.'

"'No,' said the moon. 'I like it this way. If I shine with you, no one ever notices me. But now that I shine all night by myself, everyone sees and admires me.'

"'You are a very vain, renegade moon!' the sun said angrily. 'But have your own way. I can't force you. However, if you must shine all night, will you please shine less brightly so Man can sleep, and with less heat so you do not kill Man's crops?'

"'What about you?' she answered. 'Why don't you dim your own light, if you're so concerned about poor Man?'

"'Me?' cried the sun. 'Not me!'

"'Well then, not me either!' said the moon.

"'But one of us must dim or Man cannot survive,' the sun said. Then he went on slyly, 'I'll tell you what: We'll have a race. A swimming race across the river. Whoever reaches the other side first takes the day.'

"'Done!' cried the moon, dashing for the river without waiting for a signal, cheating a head start. But the sun was quick and was upon her heels in an instant.

"When they reached the river's edge, though, Mr. Sun stopped suddenly and allowed Mrs. Moon to dive into the water all by herself. There was a long, loud hiss, and a cloud of steam rose up over the river. Above it all could be heard a piercing, sorrowful cry from Mrs. Moon.

"'Ahhhhhhhhhhhhhhhhhhhhhhhhhhhh!'

"Mrs. Moon had forgotten that she was made of fire, and fire and water do not mix. When she came out of the river, she had lost her heat. From that day on, the moon has never been hot again, and she has never shone so brightly either."

Sumu had been listening with his eyes wide. "What a good trick!" he cried. "But what a sneaky trick! What did Mrs. Moon say when she came out of the water?"

"Not one word. And no one could tell whether the water that ran down her face was river water or tears. But when she saw her husband, do you know what she did?"

"What?"

"She picked up a stick and went after him. Old Mr. Sun turned around and ran like he had hot pepper on his tail, Mrs. Moon right behind him. And she's still chasing him. That's why now the sun and moon can't keep company together, why he races across the sky and she chases after, night after day after night . . ."

". . . after day after night after day," Sumu murmured to himself, looking thoughtfully up at his moon. It was a good story, but . . .

"But, Old Pa," Sumu said finally. "Why should Mr. Sun win the day? Mrs. Moon was vain and selfish and a cheater, for true, but Mr. Sun was also vain and selfish and very, very tricky. Why should he be rewarded for being mean?"

"Because that's the way it is," the Chief said flatly.

"Hmmmmm," Sumu said. "Well, I don't know. I think maybe there's another answer. I think maybe . . ."

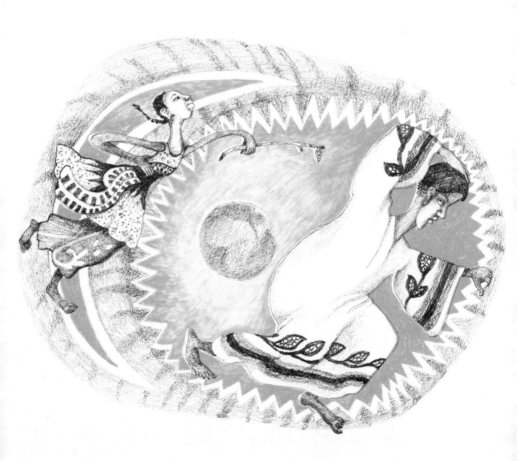

Sumu stopped when he saw the old man's sad smile, the sad, shining eyes.

"Must you have all the answers, boy?" he asked in a kind, quiet voice. "Didn't you like the story? My pa told that story to me, and his pa told it to him, and his pa before him told it to him. Isn't that enough for you?"

"But I don't understand everything yet. Shouldn't I keep asking until I have all the answers?"

The old Chief stood up with a crackling and a groan, looked up at the brilliant moon, and sighed. "I don't know. Perhaps you should. Perhaps . . ." He paused.

"Perhaps what?" Sumu asked.

"It is a very long, very hard journey, but perhaps it is time you walked with me to Banplu. There is a school there. There will be a teacher."

"Will the teacher know about the moon?" Sumu asked eagerly.

"The teacher too will have a story. My story came from our people; the teacher's story will come from a book. It will be a story of numbers, of distance and weight and measures. Perhaps it is time for you to hear it."

"Is it a true story?"

"Only you will be able to say," the Chief replied, putting his arm around Sumu's shoulder. "But whatever you decide, I know you will not forget my story, and I hope one day you will tell it to your child."

And so, because he was the Chief and always right, he convinced Sumu's ma and pa to let the boy go away to the school. Early the next morning the old man and young boy began the long walk to get at the truth about the moon.

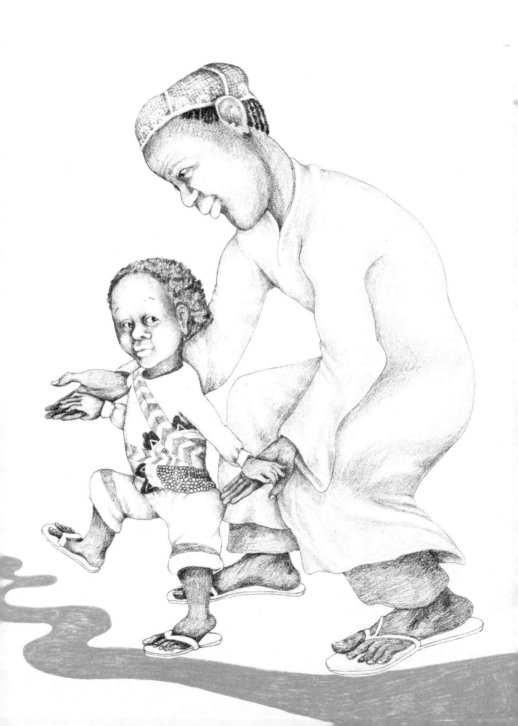

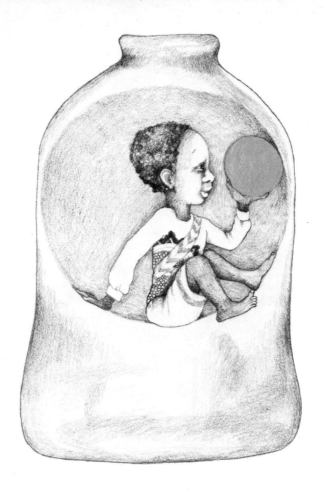

When they finally arrived, it was late in the night.
How glad and surprised Sumu was to find his
friend the moon waiting for him there, smiling
down at him all these many, lonely miles from
home. Sumu leaped and made a grab for it. He
would have it in a bottle.